# PRAISE FOR *SHAFTED*

"**Shafted** is a first-person dissection of America's trade policies. A trade policy crafted by the rich for the rich has incalculable effects on all. The poor, forgotten, and dislocated are not being heard, yet the ease with which corporations and governments ignore such suffering is a luxury even the rich cannot afford. It is imperative that we listen well, for the cost of indifference will never stop growing until these inequities are addressed and justice trumps cash as the motivating factor for economic development."

—Paul Hawken, author, *The Ecology of Commerce*

"Today in the name of 'free trade' we are losing some of our most important freedoms. This book shows how farmers, workers, and consumers are being trapped by an unjust system—and how to do something about it."

—Eric Schlosser, author, *Fast Food Nation*

"This important book gives voice to those invisible workers often missing in the free trade debate. For them the only thing free about free trade is the free-fall in their standard of living. These voices are dramatic testimony about the challenges that globalization poses, and make a case for changing the terms of globalization so that its gains are far more widely distributed. Thanks, Food First, for a volume that lifts the voices of our nation's working poor and shines light on a problem too many policymakers would rather ignore."

—Julianne Malveaux, economist and author

"The rights of the men and women who labor in our fields and orchards must be upheld by trade laws that treat them fairly, give them a voice in their working conditions, and let them maintain decent living conditions for themselves and their families. This book is important because it sheds light on the darker side of current trade agreements. It will help the American public understand that when we do negotiate more treaties, we need to ensure that they are fair, just, and equitable for all American workers."

—Congressman George Miller (D-CA)

"Ten years have passed since the North American Free Trade Agreement came into effect. It's about time this free trade regime was put on trial. Now, thanks to Food First, we have a line-up of witnesses who've experienced first hand the fall-out of free trade. They reveal how 'free' trade enshrines corporate rights over basic human rights. These voices must be heard and a corresponding verdict rendered."

—Tony Clarke, Director, Polaris Institute; co-author, *Global Showdown*

"After a decade of footing the bill for NAFTA's obscene disasters, frontline experts come to Congress mad as hornets, straight from fields, factories, and fishing boats. But they don't stop with sharing the blinding hunger, gnawing poverty, and spirit-killing wounds workers suffer thanks to free trade. Instead folks press on with concrete, practical steps for triaging the wounded and righting corporate wrongs. Thank you Christine Ahn and Food First for assembling some of our favorite fighters to show our elected officials how to better govern!"

—Miriam Ching Yoon Louie, author, *Sweatshop Warriors*

"All our lives are shaped by free trade policies. Crises of overproduction and resource depletion; decimation of small farmers by transnational agribusiness; immigration of workers to U.S. jobs that then migrate toward cheaper labor overseas: **Shafted** strikingly reveals the human costs and bitter ironies of our current trade policies.

—Linda Burnham, Executive Director,
Women of Color Resource Center

"Food First has done an extraordinary job in publishing the testimony of working Americans about the impact of free trade on America's working poor and the environment. This is powerful stuff."

—Pablo Eisenberg, Senior Fellow,
Georgetown Public Policy Institute

"This important book underscores the need for a new paradigm for negotiating international trade agreements. Under the current system, trade agreements merely send capital off in search of the lowest wage platforms. Future agreements must respect the dignity of people and lift them up."

—Congresswoman Marcy Kaptur (D-OH)

"'Free trade' doesn't just benefit the multinational corporations. It inflicts real harm to people's lives and devastating changes to families and communities across America and the world. Here are the stories of those who were its first casualties—and who later became the living proof of how a struggle for justice and democracy transforms us. In their resilience, vision, and courage, we find the strength, clarity, and urgency to bring about another world.

—Helen S. Kim, Asian Immigrant Women Advocates
and Building Movement Project

# Shafted

## FREE TRADE AND AMERICA'S WORKING POOR

Foreword by **DENNIS KUCINICH**
Introduction by **ANURADHA MITTAL**
Edited by **CHRISTINE AHN**

Food First Books
Oakland, California

Cover and text design by Stephen Hassett
Photographs by Jim Saah

ISBN 0-935028-92-7

Food First Books are distributed by:
Client Distribution Services (CDS)
425 Madison Ave, 3rd Floor, New York, NY 10017
800-343-4199
www.cdsbooks.com

Printed in the United States
5 4 3 2 1 – 03 04 05 06 07

# CONTENTS

# Foreword.

The ornately decorated, gilded conference room on Capitol Hill known appropriately as the "Gold Room" was the backdrop to an important public forum on June 12, 2003.

Farmworkers, farmers, fishermen, industrial workers, advocates, and academics came from every corner of the country to testify about the effects of international trade agreements such as NAFTA. What they said, from personal experience and footnoted research, revealed the underside of the conventional wisdom about globalization.

This book contains the testimony from that day of truth-telling. You will read about how poverty has deepened as a result of our trade agreements, about how our trade agreements have been used to further the violation of human rights, and about how workers in this country have been pitted against workers in other countries by the companies that authored and now exploit NAFTA and the WTO.

One point of view you will not read in this book is the official view from the White House. The United States Trade Representative was invited to attend. In fact, he was promised that any reasonable accommodation would be made to allow him to speak at a time convenient for him. But he chose not to respond to the invitation.

It is rare that the views of workers dominate the marble-tiled halls and wood-paneled hearing rooms of Congress. But if Congress were truly responsive to the aspirations of the majority, this book is what more congressional hearings would sound like.

Dennis J. Kucinich
Member of Congress
Co-Chair, Congressional Progressive Caucus

# Preface.

On June 12, 2003, a delegation of America's working poor gathered for a congressional briefing in Washington, D.C. Convened by the Congressional Progressive Caucus and Food First, a progressive think tank, the briefing was a rare chance for working poor people to speak collectively to members of Congress and the American public about the impact of free trade on their lives. Shafted: Free Trade and America's Working Poor is based on that briefing.

The women and men whose stories are woven into this book come from incredibly diverse ethnic backgrounds, geographic locations, and vocations. But all have experienced a variation on the destructive power of the free trade policies of the last decade. Communities and families are broken; wages wither and jobs evaporate forever; farms, houses, and livelihoods—and even lives—are lost.

When Food First began the task of identifying a delegation to testify, we weren't looking for mere victims of free trade— we wanted to bring forward communities who resisted and fought back. The people whose stories you will read are the conscience among us, the ones who spoke up and started organizing when they and their fellow workers were fired as the factory shut down and moved overseas. They are the ones who refused to believe that trade policies that forced family farms into foreclosure was progress, or inevitable. They are the ones who refused to be treated as second-class citizens without fundamental human rights. They are the champions of true American values and the leaders to whom we owe a debt for their courage in fighting to make this world more just and fair for everyone.

This book comes at a very critical juncture in history. The theory of free trade, which says that these punishing economic policies are part of a natural, fair, and self-correcting mechanism over which we have no control, is collapsing under the weight of real world experience. Yet the U.S. is pushing for more trade liberalization through the Free Trade Area of the Americas (FTAA) and the World Trade Organization (WTO). This without a national review of how NAFTA and other existing trade polices have affected the domestic economy. This book is an integral part of the global justice movement that is making the connection most of our policymakers won't: if free trade hasn't worked for America's poor—and it doesn't—it certainly won't work for the poor in developing countries.

Shafted chronicles the voices of family farmers, farmworkers, and industrial workers from across the United States and their struggle to survive under the assault of free trade. Each story in this book cites articles from the Universal Declaration of Human Rights and related covenants to help us understand how the rights and freedoms for corporations and capital dictated by free trade agreements fundamentally works against human rights. Analysts from activist, academic, labor, and state government supplement the picture with hard-hitting facts about how the U.S. has actually failed to realize the promises of free trade.

But it will take more than our becoming educated about free trade policies to counter the corporate interests that dictate our collective future. It will take action. That is why we have included an education-for-action resource section at the back of the book—to help each and every one of us mobilize to change the current system, which says that people without money have no voice and those who do don't have to care. Contact the organizations listed there to find out what they are currently working on and how you can join in the fight. Let's take back our democracy and our future. We owe it to our ancestors, who fought for our basic civil, human, and ecological rights; to those who are living without hopes and dreams; and to future generations who will preserve this great earth and all its living beings.

I'd like to thank my colleagues at Food First who made this book possible. I'd like to give special thanks to Anuradha Mittal for her tireless vision, Clancy Drake for being the most impeccable managing editor and go-to woman, Steve Hassett for generously offering his artistic talent in designing the book, and Nick Parker and Michael Manoocheri, whose immense skill and craftsmanship made the congressional briefing such a global success. This book was made possible by my dedicated interns, especially Sarah Marxer and Jen Clarke.

The congressional briefing would not have been possible,

especially in these strange political times, without the leadership of Rep. Dennis Kucinich and his chief of staff, Jaron Bourke, and the Congressional Progressive Caucus. And neither the briefing nor the book would be available to students, activists, educators, and policymakers were it not for the people who courageously testified, believing in the importance of coming together and presenting their case against free trade to members of Congress and to the American public.

I must thank my family: my mother, who bore thirteen children, raised ten, and lived through Japanese colonial occupation, the Korean War, and working-class immigrant life in America; and my sisters and brother who invested in keeping all of us housed, clothed, and fed. We must never forget where we come from and the people who have touched our lives.

—Christine Ahn

# Introduction.

## "Free" Trade Is a Human Rights Calamity
### BY ANURADHA MITTAL

President Franklin Roosevelt told Americans in 1944 that true individual freedom cannot exist without economic security and independence. Calling for a "second bill of rights" to establish a new basis of security and prosperity for all, he argued that people who are hungry and out of work are the stuff of which dictatorships are made.

In 1948, the Universal Declaration of Human Rights (UDHR) was adopted by the General Assembly of the United Nations. A cornerstone for human rights, Article 25 of the Universal Declaration of Human Rights guaranteed everyone "the right to a standard of living adequate for the health and well-being of himself (herself) and of his (her) family, including food, clothing, housing, and medical care and necessary social services, and the right to security in the event of unemployment, sickness, disability, widowhood, old age, or other lack of livelihood in circumstances beyond his (her) control."

The UDHR provided governments with a set of guiding principles, and was codified through human rights conventions and covenants that are legally binding. It is this framework of international human rights we should use to judge the impact of free trade agreements on our lives and communities.

On January 1, 1994, the North American Free Trade Agreement (NAFTA) was implemented, joining Mexico, Canada, and the U.S. into a common market to create the largest free trade area in the world, covering (at the time) some 360 million people. Meanwhile, negotiations to create the World Trade Organization (WTO) resulted in that organization's rules taking effect on January 1, 1995. Now talks are on for the Free Trade Area of the Americas (FTAA), which will create a single market from Alaska to Patagonia, including every country in the hemisphere except Cuba and integrating all into the global economy.

The proponents of NAFTA, as of all trade agreements, promised it would raise standards of living and ensure full employment in the context of expanding trade, while upholding the objective of sustainable development. The truth is that NAFTA has sparked a race to the bottom of wages, employment, and working conditions, where workers in every NAFTA country have suffered. NAFTA was to bring over 200,000 new jobs each year to Americans. Between 1994 and 2000, the U.S. experienced a net loss of 3.2 million jobs. In one ten-month period, between September 2000 and June 2001, 675,000 jobs were eliminated in the manufacturing sector alone. These were generally union jobs with decent pay and benefits, and their loss left workers to find new work that paid only 70 percent of their former salary.

It is "cost-effective" for footloose corporations to move their operations to Mexico, home to over 2,700 *maquiladoras* (assembly sweatshops producing for export) since 1994. These factories employ over 1.3 million Mexican workers, mostly young women, who are paid on average 50 cents an hour, have no job security or benefits, and are often subject to sexual harassment and unsafe working conditions. The suffering of workers in both the U.S. and Mexico is not an anomaly of NAFTA: it is free trade's logical outcome.

Successive administrations assert that free trade helps America's farmers, and therefore it helps Americans. A comparison between the state of U.S. farmers in the 1930s and their position today dismantles that myth. In the 1930s, 25 percent of the population lived on the nation's 6 million farms; today, our 2 million farms are home to 2 percent of the population. An average farming household today earns only 13 percent of its income from agriculture and the rest from a second and third job. Rates of depression and suicide in our farming communities have increased at an alarming rate. The U.S. has captured world markets through low commodity prices, with the result that one out of three acres planted in the United States produces food or fiber destined for export— much of it sold at below the farmer's cost of production. For example, the U.S. exports corn at prices 20 percent below the cost of production, and wheat at 46 percent below cost. Practically the only producers that can survive in this situation are big agribusiness farms that garner the overwhelming majority of government subsidies. So U.S. taxpayers keep big producers afloat, small farmers can't compete and disappear, and the low farm commodity prices that free trade fosters only increase the profits of processors, exporters, and seed and chemical companies.

Small farmers in the rest of North America can't compete either: cheap subsidized agricultural products dumped on their markets have devastated their livelihoods and communities as well. Six hundred farmers lose their land each day in Mexico and head to the U.S., where they find death or incarceration at the border, or a job in a sweatshop, or work as a day laborer, or enslavement in the fields, working twelve to thirteen hours a day, six days a week, to earn $20.

Free trade is not free. It has shackled our communities, stifled our voices, and threatened to do away with our human rights. Workers, in spite of being the most necessary element of society, are being robbed of their labor and deprived of their elementary rights. The peasant who grows corn for all starves with her family; the garment factory worker who supplies the world market with clothes has not enough to cover her own and her children's bodies; masons, smiths, and carpenters who raise magnificent palaces live like pariahs in the ghettos. The corporations that profit from all this labor squander millions on whims. These terrible inequalities, and the forced disparity of economic chances and choices, make it obvious that the present order of society is built on the brink of a volcano.

That volcano is erupting. On January 1, 1994, the inauguration of NAFTA was answered by the uprising of the Zapatista Army of National Liberation (EZLN) in Chiapas. Since then, millions of people have taken to the streets in

India, the Philippines, Indonesia, Brazil, Venezuela, Australia, South Africa, Europe—everywhere—in massive demonstrations to show their outrage against the free trade paradigm.

Unified by a commitment to universal values of democracy, social and economic justice, peace, and respect for life and human dignity, the global justice movement that has come together cannot be merely identified as an "anti-globalization" movement. It is the global movement for justice, for women's rights, for immigrant and indigenous peoples' rights, for workers' and farmers' rights. It is the movement with the conviction that a better world is possible and the alternatives that will bring it into being. This new human rights movement is an open challenge to the lies of free trade agreements.

*Shafted: Free Trade and America's Working Poor* encompasses the voices of the activists that form this movement in the United States. Each personal testimonial is a voice for thousands and speaks to the will of millions. Tearing apart the myth of free trade for the working poor, these people's battle cry is the same as Zapatistas': "we demand our right to human dignity, and our basic human rights—the right to food, housing...and an adequate standard of living." Finally, Shafted is not a litany of victimization: it is a call for revolution, and a permanent testament to human courage and the human spirit that fights back against all injustice.

# 1.
# Farm
# ers.

"In reality, the only winners are the multinational food and grain processing and exporting companies.

**KEITH DITTRICH**
American Corn Growers Association

I am Keith J. Dittrich, a corn and soybean farmer from Tilden, Nebraska and also president of the American Corn Growers Association (ACGA). The ACGA represents 14,000 corn producers and was formed in 1987 after our dissatisfaction with organizations that represented corn producers during the landmark 1985 farm bill debate. Trade was a key focus of this debate and much of the emphasis of that farm bill was focused on adjusting farm policy to allow farmers to be "more competitive in the global marketplace." The theory was that if we would reduce price support mechanisms for basic commodities (which in turn would reduce market prices), farmers would benefit from increased commodity exports and reduced burdensome grain stocks.

To the supporters of this concept, principally the multinational grain processing and exporting companies, the bill was not an entire success. They had hoped for a complete "decoupling" of farm programs from production that would allow for all-out production on the farm, providing them with large quantities of commodities at low prices, due to the elimination of all price support mechanisms.

The ACGA understood that congressional intent would likely be circumvented to further reduce farm policy price impacting mechanisms through the General Agreement on Tariffs and Trade (GATT), which is now the World Trade Organization (WTO). This would be achieved by making domestic farm programs that affected price or managed supply "illegal" under WTO rules. Our first director of congressional affairs, Mr. John Ford, who had served as an undersecretary of agriculture and chief liaison between Congress and the Reagan administration, testified to this numerous times as he warned of the true intent of such free trade agreements.

After the 1985 farm legislation passed, it was apparent that farm and trade policy experts were focusing on the upcoming GATT negotiations, with the intent of reducing farm subsidies worldwide through liberalized trade to the supposed benefit of farmers here and abroad.

Early in the process, ACGA assessed the dramatic effects on U.S. agriculture if reductions in domestic farm programs were made under the auspices of trade liberalization. First of all, we knew that exports of basic commodities were relatively inelastic, and secondly, that reductions and the elimination of price support mechanisms, such as grain reserves and acreage idling programs, would have devastating effects on family farmers here and abroad. We sounded the alarms far and wide of what would happen if such a course were followed, but apparently this fell on deaf ears.

The United States has continued to liberalize trade and radically adjust farm programs, which has led to the devastation of rural America. In my home community, radical changes have taken place as family farm operations have either had to expand to survive or seek off-farm jobs to make ends meet. Currently, our rural communities in Nebraska are facing severe education budget shortfalls that threaten to close many schools down. The infrastructure has either degraded or stagnated since these trade agreements have passed.

Our local community has also seen a large influx of foreign workers now employed in meatpacking plants who have come because of the lack of jobs and opportunity in their home countries. Some of them are farmers who have been displaced by the same trade agreements that were supposed to improve their lives. This influx has caused severe societal problems for our communities as several different cultures are forced to merge in a very short time.

The 2002 farm bill, although slightly improved, fails to improve commodity prices through the reinstatement of historically proven price impacting mechanisms, since many of these are considered "illegal" in the eyes of the WTO.[1] Proponents of a decoupled approach to farm programs have been very successful over the last eighteen years in achieving their goals through trade agreements, which have very limited congressional oversight.

Progress toward the stated goals of trade agreements and of the past four farm bills—to expand trade and improve the incomes of farmers—has been dismal at the best. For instance, exports of corn have stayed nearly static over the eighteen-year period while average market prices are 40 percent lower than what they were in the early 1980s, even adjusting for inflation. Again, this dramatic reduction in farm gate prices has driven thousands of farmers off the land and caused many rural communities to collapse due to a depressed farm economy.

Since trade liberalization's effects were so damaging to U.S. producers, one would think that the winners were farm-

---

1 For an analysis of the impact of the 2002 farm bill, see Anuradha Mittal, "Giving Away the Farm: The 2002 Farm Bill," *Food First Backgrounder 8(3)*, Summer 2002, at *www.foodfirst.org*.

ers from other nations, who supposedly have better access to markets through trade liberalization. To the contrary, farmers around the world have suffered along with U.S. farmers as commodity prices fell globally. Many have suffered even more seriously than U.S. producers due to the lack of any income assistance, which we did have.

Even consumers have failed to benefit from reduced commodity prices. Data show that retail consumer food prices have increased by nearly 250 percent over a twenty-five-year period, while commodity prices paid to farmers have remained flat or have decreased. Beginning in 1985, changes in the farm bill transferred the cost of commodities from the consumer to the taxpayer. In 1985 the cost of the farm bill jumped from a mere few billion a year to over $26 billion, and now exceeds $30 billion annually.

In reality, the only winners are the multinational food and grain processing and exporting companies. These companies have also dramatically shifted our livestock production to vertically integrated systems controlled solely by them. They have achieved their goals of ensuring plentiful low cost commodities to process, transport, and sell around the world at the expense of farmers, laborers, taxpayers, and consumers.

---

**EVERYONE HAS THE RIGHT TO WORK, TO FREE CHOICE OF EMPLOYMENT...AND TO PROTECTION AGAINST UNEMPLOYMENT.**

— Article 23, Universal Declaration of Human Rights

**Farm families have become pawns in a dangerous game played by powerful people who trade away the futures of the next generations.**

DENA HOFF
National Family Farm Coalition

I am a family farmer from eastern Montana and a member of the National Family Farm Coalition, which was founded to bring together farmers and others to strengthen family farms and rural communities.

Free trade is no longer about an exchange of commodities between countries—wheat for coffee or bananas. What free trade is really about is procuring the unregulated movement of unlimited amounts of capital anywhere in the world. To this end, farm families have become pawns in a dangerous game played by powerful people who trade away the futures of the next generations of farm families, who in turn neither understand nor consent to the rules of the game.

When Congress gives up the right to debate and amend trade agreements, they stop any meaningful participation by the American people in decisions that will affect every facet of their lives as well as the lives of every person on this planet.

Free trade is no longer an economic issue. It is a moral issue. Valuing trade over all, including citizens' right to participate in trade decisions and to hope that free trade can be fair trade, is wrong.

Will U.S. trade policy mean that farm prices will be above the cost of production for all farmers worldwide? Will countries have the right to determine domestic food and farm policies to benefit their own citizens? Will there be family farms for my own children and other farm children who want to farm? Will countries have the right to protect the public health and welfare of their citizens if their regulations deny a profit to a corporation?

Unless you can answer an unequivocal yes to each question, something is morally wrong with our current trade policy.

In the nearly ten years since NAFTA, the facts show that the impacts to family farmers and ranchers in the U.S., Canada, and Mexico have been disastrous. Yet we stand ready to export this disaster to the rest of the Western Hemisphere.

I urge you, for the sake of a healthy rural America, to finally lift up your voices and say what family farmers have known for nearly ten years of NAFTA—the emperor has no clothes!

A trade policy that is secret and undemocratic and that ignores the impacts on family farms, workers, and the environment is a slap in the face to every American who believes he or she lives in a country that proclaims liberty and justice for all.

Please take a hard look at all we stand to lose as a people and as a nation. Review the broken promises of NAFTA and pledge to work for fair trade agreements negotiated for the good of all. Our future depends on your commitment to making all trade fair trade.

---

**THE WILL OF THE PEOPLE SHALL BE THE BASIS OF THE AUTHORITY OF GOVERNMENT.**

— Article 21, Universal Declaration of Human Rights

" We small farmers beg our government for a chance to simply exist. "

**GARY GRANT**
Black Farmers and Agriculturalists Association

I am a former small family farmer from North Carolina, and president of the Black Farmers and Agriculturalists Association (BFAA). On our farm, we planted row crops, such as cotton, tobacco, corn, soybeans, and wheat.

Black family farmers and the Black rural community have suffered under U.S. agriculture policies that promote corporate concentration and exports through free trade agreements. We are the canary in the mineshaft of American agriculture, and what has happened to Black family farmers in this country is what is now happening to the small family farmer in America.

In 1910, Black farmers owned between 16 and 19 million acres, and by 1997, we collectively owned just 1.5 million acres. Twenty years ago, there were 50,000 Black-operated family farms in the U.S., and today there are just over 10,000. My family's struggle to stay on the farm is the same as my parents'. Like many farm families, they left the city with their five young children to realize their dreams of independence and their love for the land.

In the 1950s, we lived in the New Deal resettlement community of Tillery, North Carolina with 300 other Black farming families. Today, none of those farmers are farming. Large White farmers are now tending 98 percent of that farmland. My parents worked sixteen hours a day, seven days a week as small farmers, and my dad worked weekends as a barber. Even though they worked so hard, institutional racism prevented them from staying on the land, and in 1976, their farm went into foreclosure. The destruction of our farm led to high levels of stress and the deterioration of their health, which led to my parents' early death. Our family is just one example of what has happened to the rest of the Black farmers.

In 1997, in a civil rights action report, the USDA admitted it had systematically discriminated against Black farmers. The following year, the Pigford v. Glickman case, in which Black farmers sought monetary compensation and debt relief for the discrimination and racism they endured from 1981 through 1996, was declared a class action lawsuit. Although over 100,000 Black farmers have sought to become a part of the class action lawsuit, only 21,591 have been accepted into the lawsuit, and as of December 2002 only 12,972 have actually received any compensation. The majority of those who have received a settlement have not been able to return to farming or reclaim their land.

The BFAA farmers and small Black farmers in the Pigford lawsuit are so weary from the fight with our government, of standing in welfare lines for a few food stamps to feed ourselves, of having to turn to working in local sweatshops to keep a roof over our heads, of having to spend our retirement years on another welfare check called Supplemental Social Security, and from suffering from diabetes, heart disease, and high blood pressure.

Discrimination destroyed the ability of Black farmers to survive. The funding for loans that were denied to Black farmers did not sit idly by. It was used. For every dollar that did not find its way into a Black farmer's operation, a dollar did find its way into a White farmer's operation. In a world of limited financial resources, denial of access and support for one group usually means heightened access and support for another. With resources getting tighter and the destruction of Black farmers so thorough and complete, small White farmers were next.

U.S. agricultural policy believes that Archer Daniels Midland (ADM) can feed a hungry world, and even worse, that they can do it better than a robust mixture of vibrant family farmers. In effect, the government subsidizes large corporate giants like ADM, Monsanto, and Tyson, which doesn't reduce hunger in the world, but increases the inequitable distribution of wealth, with wealth trickling upward and away from small family farmers.

The U.S. has implemented trade agreements that are supposed to establish a "fair playing field" and open international markets. Without a doubt, small farmers view these trade agreements as more elaborate mechanisms to cheat ordinary farmers and the people out of their fair share.

The free trade strategies of the U.S. government have destroyed and eradicated small farmers and rural development and employment. We do know that replacing small farmers with the large agricultural complex, with the goal of exporting crops, does nothing to increase America's rural employment or broaden the distribution of income and strategies of nonfarm rural enterprises. It breaks the human spirit of America's family farmers, and is the root and fundamental cause of poverty, disease, ignorance, and injustice in rural America, and in rural Black America in particular.

There is no single formula for saving small farmers and their generations of knowledge, and for achieving rural development. However, we do know that with the right government help and investment, small farmers don't have to perish and be deprived of what they enjoy most—being stewards of the land. They don't have to be subjected to poor mental health and an array of terminal diseases. Rural educational systems don't have to be diminished and compromised. The abject out-migration of most of our young people doesn't have to happen, and small towns don't have to die in isolation—all because of subsistence farming, and because government policies help large corporate agriculture.

We small farmers beg our own government for a chance to simply exist; beg to simply take part in the American dream of ownership, work, and giving back. There has got to be a better way to keep the work and the sacrifices of small farmers from being so trivialized, and our worth and performance as citizens from becoming so second-class.

THE LAW SHALL PROHIBIT
ANY DISCRIMINATION AND GUARANTEE TO ALL
PERSONS EQUAL AND EFFECTIVE PROTECTION
AGAINST DISCRIMINATION ON ANY
GROUND SUCH AS RACE, COLOR, SEX,
LANGUAGE, RELIGION, POLITICAL OR OTHER
OPINION, NATIONAL OR SOCIAL ORIGIN,
PROPERTY, BIRTH, OR OTHER STATUS.
— Article 26, International Covenant on Civil and
Political Rights

"We need to understand that the American dairy farmer is not suffering from competition. We are suffering from a kind of cannibalism. We have the gluttons of concentrated power devouring the American dairy farmer in the name of free trade."

JOHN BUNTING
Dairy Farmer

I am a dairy farmer in Delhi, New York, in the western foothills of the Catskill Mountains. At one time, Delaware County, New York, was called the "Kingdom of the Cow." The town of Bovina was named to honor the main economic activity of the area.

We have a milking herd of thirty-five Jersey cows. Each cow has a name. Our cows roam and eat freely from a different section of pasture each day during the grazing season. We have repeatedly won awards for the quality of our milk. In short, we farm in the manner that virtually every American prefers.

Our local landscape limits the scale of farming. For a very long time, this meant the practice of farming was mutually beneficial to people and the environment. Steadily, though, the numbers of farms in our area has dwindled. Farming in cooperation with nature is thought to be a thing of the past. Exploiting nature through increased scale is called "efficient" by land grant experts.

Those of us who continue to dairy farm in Delaware County have learned to cut costs to the bone. We fix our aging equipment. We have virtually become our own veterinarians. Our success, if surviving can be called success, is obtained from our skills and our stubbornness.

Dairy farmers are failing now in spite of every effort. Milk prices have continued at record lows for over a year. Many of us feel betrayed. In other parts of the state and the country, those who have gotten big upon the advice of experts feel an even greater sense of betrayal. There are record levels of foreclosures throughout the country.

While dairy farmers are seeing record low milk prices, imports of dairy products have poured in from all over the globe.

Cheese is coming from countries unknown for cheese production. Lithuania is now the fifth-largest exporter of cheese. We import from there a type of cheese called Goya. It has no tariff rate quota and when grated is indistinguishable from Italian type grated cheese. It is imported for about 42 percent of the cost of cheese from Italy.

If you consider the imports of powdered dairy products, you see the global corporate hand reaching to countries around the globe. There has been a steady increase of imported dairy proteins from India. We have increased our imports of caseinates from China this year. Dairy powders are coming from Russia, Belarus, and Ukraine. It is a known fact that milk from that part of the world is commonly contaminated with persistent radioactive residue from Chernobyl. Any in-depth analysis of dairy imports shows a growing trend toward increasing risk.

All of this occurs because of price. U.S. dairy farmers cannot compete. And with barely more than 1 percent of Americans farming, we have become a nation disconnected from a working knowledge of our food supply. The level of tragedy and depression on American dairy farms is gut-wrenching. Our hope has all but disappeared.

Generating sympathy, however, is merely a distraction from the real problem. We are where we are today not because of any Darwinian progress of economics. We need to understand that this current tragedy is the result of choices made in corporate boardrooms. We need to understand that the American dairy farmer is not suffering from competition. We are suffering from a kind of cannibalism. We have the gluttons of concentrated power devouring the American dairy farmer in the name of free trade.

EVERY PERSON HAS THE RIGHT TO THE
PRESERVATION OF HIS HEALTH
THROUGH SANITARY AND SOCIAL MEASURES
RELATING TO FOOD, CLOTHING, HOUSING,
AND MEDICAL CARE, TO THE EXTENT
PERMITTED BY PUBLIC AND COMMUNITY
RESOURCES.

— Article 11, American Declaration of the Rights and Duties of Man

# The World Trade Organization (WTO) has held that many conservation measures are 'impediments to trade' and has struck them down.

## PIETRO PARRAVANO
Pacific Coast Federation of Fishermen's Associations

I am a commercial fisherman from the small port of Half Moon Bay in California, just south of San Francisco. I operate my boat alone or with one crewmember, fishing for salmon, crab, and rockfish, and with my wife I sell our catch at local farmer's markets on weekends. For over ten years, I have served as president of the Pacific Coast Federation of Fishermen's Associations (PCFFA), the U.S. West Coast's largest commercial fishermen's organization, representing small- to midsize-vessel, fishing family owner-operators. I also serve as a U.S. delegate to the World Forum of Fish Harvesters and Fishworkers and have had the privilege of serving as one of two commercial fishermen representatives on the Pew Oceans Commission.

The media has been filled over the past few years with stories of our oceans being in trouble, fisheries in collapse, listing of fish stocks under the Endangered Species Act, and fishing imperiling the ocean environment. As a member of the Pew Commission, I have had a chance to see firsthand many of the problems facing our fisheries and, in turn, our fishing communities. Coastal development, pollution, certain fishing practices and types of aquaculture, invasive species, and habitat loss all threaten our oceans, our fisheries, the livelihoods of fishing men and women, and coastal economies.

There is another threat to our nation's fisheries, and indeed to fishing families and communities throughout the globe. You see, not all of our fisheries are in trouble. Some are very healthy. On the West Coast, for example, salmon in Alaska are abundant and even many of our king salmon runs in California and the Pacific Northwest are plentiful, despite the listings of numerous Pacific salmon runs. Pacific and California halibut, sablefish, squid, sardines, sand dabs, Dungeness crab, California lobster, pink shrimp, and albacore tuna are in good shape, in large measure because of the vigilance and stewardship of fishing men and women working in concert with fishery agencies and conservation groups. But even the best of our fisheries and those who depend on them are now at risk because of free trade agreements.

The threat of cheap imports is not something far off in the future. Our markets for wild salmon have largely collapsed due to the flood of farmed fish imports. These farmed salmon operations are mostly owned by a few large European corporations that have been successful in externalizing their true costs of production, making the public pay for the environmental damage these operations cause—never mind the potential human health risks some of these aquacultured products present because of the use of antibiotics, pesticides, and food colorings in fish farms.

Cheap farmed salmon has driven down the price paid to fishermen for wild salmon to the point many can no longer break even, even in Alaska where salmon runs have been exceptional. As a result fishermen are selling out, if they can even find buyers for their boats and permits. Processing plants are closing and the fishing infrastructure of so many of our coastal communities is beginning to collapse. With this have come the social problems we have seen elsewhere when basic industries collapse: people are thrown out of work, and communities lose hope. In fact, the governor of Alaska declared the state an economic disaster two years ago.

The shrimp fishery in the Southeast and Gulf is suffering a similar plight with the flood of cheap farmed shrimp imports from China and elsewhere. Cheap imports, mostly farmed fish products from nations that either directly subsidize fish farming or indirectly subsidize it by allowing operators to externalize costs, are just one problem facing fishing men and women from increased globalization.

U.S. fishermen are required under U.S. law to follow stringent conservation measures to protect fish stocks, other marine life, and ocean ecosystems. This is an acceptable standard, but it does come at a cost. This would not be a problem if we were competing with fish from other nations abiding by the same conservation and management standards, but we are not. The World Trade Organization (WTO) has held that many conservation measures are "impediments to trade" and has struck them down. Thus, U.S. fishermen have to abide by stringent conservation measures—which we believe in—but our competitors do not, thereby placing us at a competitive disadvantage.

Another issue we worry about is how the WTO will define subsidies. Certainly my organization and many others deplore subsidies that create overcapitalization in the fishing fleet. Nor can we afford to have the WTO classify as "subsidies" fishery mitigation measures, such as those to offset the impacts of dams or logging—particularly at a time when we're trying to recover Endangered Species Act–listed stocks.

Last year's farm bill requires country-of-origin labeling and, for fish, a requirement that they be labeled as "wild" or "farmed." Those types of national labeling requirements, including even FDA requirements for labeling fish with food coloring or state requirements for labeling fish for mercury content, could be viewed by the WTO as trade impediments. But good labeling not only helps consumers, it helps conscientious fishermen working to fish sustainably and bring to market a nutritious product.

As you are aware, there is a big push among some large chemical and biotech firms to promote genetically modified food products. It's not just soy or corn. Transgenic fish are on their way. Even if nations or states decide to prohibit or control genetically engineered fish to protect native natural stocks or the environment, the WTO could overrule them. Who elected the WTO?

Fishing is America's oldest industry; there were commercial fishermen fishing off the Eastern seaboard before Cabot arrived. Fishing is a very special way of life and our fishing communities are special places, but I fear it is not going to be overfishing or even pollution that could end our 10,000-year-old profession. Instead, it will be destroyed by some badly crafted trade laws pushed by large corporations and banks pursuing their narrow vision of globalization.

---

**EVERYONE IS ENTITLED TO A SOCIAL AND INTERNATIONAL ORDER IN WHICH THE RIGHTS AND FREEDOMS SET FORTH IN THIS DECLARATION CAN BE FULLY REALIZED.**
— Article 28, Universal Declaration of Human Rights

2
Work
ers.

**"We can continue down a path of tension, inequality, and an assault on workers' rights or we can choose a new path of cooperation, justice, and equality."**

**KENNY RILEY**
International Longshoremen's Association

I am the president of Local 1422 of the International Longshoremen's Association (ILA). I was born, raised, and educated in Charleston, South Carolina, and I have been a longshoreman there for the past twenty-seven years. Our local represents over 1,000 longshoremen in South Carolina, which is the second-largest port on the East Coast. We are part of the 55,000-strong ILA, spanning the East Coast of the United States, Canada, and Puerto Rico.

Let me begin by stating that the ILA is not opposed to trade. Ninety-five percent of the world's commerce travels by ship. International trade is our main staple. As commerce moves into the port, we are the men along the shore who are there to receive the cargo. Therefore, as trade increases, the demand for our work grows, and jobs are created for longshoremen. But we certainly do not support "free" trade as it currently stands.

Free trade benefits industries that take advantage of cheap labor and of weakened labor and environmental laws abroad, while disadvantaging domestic competition and American workers. We, and our fellow trade unionists around the world, have felt the effects of weakened labor protections such as the basic right to association and organize. I would like to share with you a story about a clear case of union busting our local experienced three years ago.

In January 2000, 150 of our predominantly African-American dockworkers went to the port to establish a picket line to protest the Denmark-based shipping company Nordana's employment of nonunion contractors. For twenty-two years, ILA longshoremen had worked the Nordana's ships, even offering rate reductions to keep their business. When Nordana turned to nonunion labor, many ILA members felt betrayed.

Our dockworkers were met by more than 600 police officers armed in riot gear, with armored cars, armored horses, and attack dogs reminiscent of those unleashed against civil rights marchers in the 1960s, and with helicopters, police patrol boats, concussion grenades, tear gas, and rubber bullets. As I tried to calm the situation, a police officer lunged out of formation to club me, which set off another vicious and unprovoked attack by the police. We tried to defend ourselves from being clubbed to death, but we were savagely beaten.

Eight union members were arrested and charged by local officials with minor offenses; the charges were soon dropped. However, South Carolina Attorney General Charlie Condon intervened and convened a secret grand jury, which delivered a judgment charging five of our dockworkers with felony rioting and conspiracy to riot.

For nearly two years, five of our dockworkers, who became internationally known as the "Charleston 5"—Jason Edgerton, Elijah Ford, Ricky Simmons, Kenneth Jefferson, and Peter Washington—lived under house arrest. They, along with their families, endured court-imposed curfews, whereby they were prohibited from leaving their homes between the hours of 7.00 P.M. and 7:00 A.M. except to go to work or to union meetings. Furthermore, they faced up to five years in prison.

Today, the two Carolinas boast the lowest rate of unionization in the entire United States. South Carolina is a haven for giant corporations like BMW, General Electric, and Dupont for a number of reasons: only 3.7 percent of the workers are unionized; it is one of two states that do not comply with the federal minimum wage law; wages are 20 percent lower than the national average; and South Carolina boasts the best tax exemption laws for big businesses. The big corporations feared that a victory for the ILA at Nordana would spread to other corporate giants, thereby uniting working class Blacks with Whites to change the landscape of low-wage nonunion labor that has been the attraction for "runaway" industries in South Carolina.

A broad coalition of unions, support committees, faith communities, and civil rights organizations from across the country and internationally mounted a legal and education campaign supporting the Charleston 5 and the struggle for workers' rights and free speech. Thanks to their incredible financial and moral support, in November 2001, the Charleston 5 were finally freed, signaling a huge victory not only for the fundamental rights of working men and women on the docks in South Carolina, but in the United States and around the world.

This journey has taught us that we are a part of something much bigger, something that spans oceans and bridges cultures. We are part of an international labor and peoples' movement, and we must oppose free trade agreements that strengthen the rights and profits of multinational corporations on the backs of the world's workers.

We can continue down a path of tension, inequality, and an assault on workers' rights or we can choose a new path of cooperation, justice, and equality. At risk are the rights to join or form a union, and the right to protect our livelihoods and preserve a standard of living for ourselves and our families. These rights are at the core of our society, and the American labor and civil rights movements will not rest until justice is served.

---

**EVERYONE SHALL HAVE...THE RIGHT TO FORM AND JOIN TRADE UNIONS FOR THE PROTECTION OF HIS INTERESTS.**
— Article 22, International Covenant on Civil and Political Rights

"We sometimes say that poverty exists in Third World countries, but I now know that poverty exists here as well. The U.S. is not immune to poverty."

**PETRA MATA**
Fuerza Unida

**M**y name is Petra Mata. I was born in Mexico. I have completed no more than the sixth grade in school. In 1969, my husband and I came to the U.S. believing we would find better opportunities for our children and ourselves. We first arrived without documents, then became legal, and finally became citizens. For years I moved from job to job until I was employed in 1976 by the most popular company in the market, Levi Strauss & Company. I earned $9.73 an hour and also had vacation and sick leave. Levi's provided me and my family with a stable situation, and in return I was a loyal employee and worked there for fourteen years.

On January 16, 1990, Levi's closed its plant in San Antonio, Texas, where I had been working, leaving 1,150 workers unemployed, a majority of whom were Mexican-American women. The company moved its factory to Costa Rica. The closing of the plant had a strong negative effect on my life because my dream was destroyed. The biggest surprise was being fired without notice. Because of this, I say that I was, so to speak, the first survivor of free trade.

Levi's offered a severance package that included three months of health care, one week pay for each year worked, and job training. Levi's gave San Antonio $1 million for job-training programs. The job-training centers assessed our abilities to help us get training to get employed. They put everyone together in a big room and gave us a test. Everyone flunked, and so they decided that the only jobs that we qualified for were janitorial work and housekeeping. They asked interrogating questions about our personal lives. We were traumatized by the whole experience.

I decided to get my GED. But when I attended class, there was no teacher and no books. It was clear that the city was not prepared to handle these job-training programs. They had to rent buildings, which were in really bad condition. In one of the classes I attended, the roof collapsed on one of the students. I was frustrated by the amount of energy I had to put into this class for so little in return.

As a result of being laid off, I personally lost my house, my method of transportation, and the tranquility of my home. My family and I had to face new problems. My husband was forced to look for a second job on top of the one he already had. He worked from seven in the morning to six at night. Our reality was very difficult. At that time, I had not the slightest idea what free trade was or meant.

As a consequence of the plant's closing, twenty-three of the workers formed Fuerza Unida on February 12, 1990. The rest of the workers quickly joined the fight, and by the end of March we had 650 members from the same plant. Levi's had already closed twenty-six other plants throughout the country.

When we formed Fuerza Unida, I had no idea how long and hard this fight would be. No Levi's worker had ever organized before this. In forming Fuerza Unida, our mission was and continues to be to educate, empower, and organize workers to turn into promoters of social change, organizers of economic justice, and participants in a democratic process.

Free trade has left us without work, exploited, with low salaries, separated from our families, and divided within our communities. All of this has contributed to workers finding themselves more and more every day in a state of exploitation and poverty. Our basic workers' rights have been violated. We sometimes say that poverty exists in Third World countries, but I now know that poverty exists here as well. The U.S. is not immune to poverty.

Free trade's impacts are felt on a global scale. In the procession of years its influence has extended past our hemisphere to countries in Asia and Africa. Our governments make agreements behind closed doors without participation from the working persons who are most affected by these decisions—decisions that to my knowledge only benefit large corporations and those in positions of power.

My fellow worker, Viola Casares, and I understand this power dynamic because we have experienced it, we have studied it, and we have participated in delegations for Summit of the Americas, Speakers' Rally Tour in Quebec, United Nations World Conference Against Racism in South Africa, the Another World Is Possible Summit in Brazil, and the Binational Forum of NGOs in Monterrey, Mexico. These experiences have given us the opportunity to learn and to understand the struggle shared by workers and laborers in other countries also affected by free trade. It is crucial that workers of the world unite to protect our human rights!

---

EVERYONE HAS THE RIGHT TO WORK,
TO FREE CHOICE OF EMPLOYMENT...
AND TO PROTECTION AGAINST UNEMPLOYMENT.
— Article 23, Universal Declaration of Human Rights

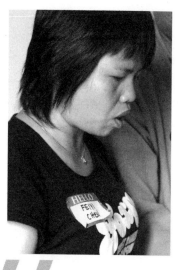

## "There are a lot of garment workers who still work ten hours a day but make less than thirty dollars a day."

**FEIYI CHEN**
Chinese Progressive Association

My name is Feiyi Chen. I immigrated to the United States in December 1998 from China. I began my working career as a seamstress in a garment factory because I did not speak English and the garment manufacturing industry was one of the few employment opportunities available to me. I typically worked ten hours a day, six days a week, at a backbreaking pace. Most garment bosses know that new immigrants have few choices when it comes to work and so they take advantage by paying workers less than the minimum wage with no overtime pay. In my case, the boss refused to pay me until I had worked in the factory for two months, and when he did pay I only got one month's worth of wages. Although I am a new immigrant, I learned from some of the older garment workers that garment workers in San Francisco actually made a decent living before free trade lured many of the better-paying garment factories over to other countries and forced the smaller and rule-abiding factories to shut down because they could not compete with the low cost of production from neighboring countries.

Because of the poor working conditions, I left the garment shop and became an electronics assembly worker in San Francisco. Although the working conditions and pay were not very good, it was better than being a seamstress because at least workers were paid minimum wage by the hour. And the lucky few who got classified as permanent workers would get some health and dental insurance coverage.

Life was still very difficult, but at least it was a stable job. However, this stability did not last long, because in September of 2001 the manager of the factory packed over

250 of the assembly workers into a room and, without warning, told us that this was our last day of work and we were to leave the premises after signing a contract to waive all claims against the company, and even our right to receive unemployment. Because the factory had us work overtime in the months prior to the layoff and we knew that there were a lot of orders in the pipeline, we asked the managers why we were being laid off. All the manager said was that it was too expensive to produce in the U.S. and that the work would be shipped overseas.

Working as a seamstress and an assembly worker has always been hard, but with so many of the factories leaving the country in search of cheaper labor, life for immigrant workers like myself is getting worse. For example, many garment workers who were paid one dollar for sewing a piece of clothing are now only making fifty cents for the same amount of work. There are a lot of garment workers who still work ten hours a day but make less than thirty dollars a day. It is getting to a point where many immigrant workers cannot afford to pay for the basic necessities of life, and increasingly I see families of four or five living in a single room with no private bathroom or kitchen because they cannot afford to rent anything else.

Since losing my job in 2001, I have been unsuccessful in finding a stable full-time job. I am not alone; just in the past two years I have met hundreds of other immigrant workers in San Francisco who have become unemployed and are unable to find work that will support a family. To survive, most workers are now forced to depend on seasonal jobs during the summer and Christmas seasons, trying to make ends meet during the rest of the year through several unstable part-time jobs like garment work, house cleaning, and restaurant work.

Although I have seen on television many American politicians claim that free trade will benefit the working poor, all I have experienced is the failure of free trade. These trade agreements have not made life better for the average American worker, and they help exploit immigrant workers. I urge the members of Congress to evaluate the impact of free trade policy on workers, and hope that our leaders will take necessary actions not only to ensure the health of corporations, but also to meet the needs of the people and attend to the welfare of all working families.

EVERYONE HAS THE RIGHT TO A STANDARD
OF LIVING ADEQUATE FOR THE
HEALTH AND WELL BEING OF HIMSELF AND OF
HIS FAMILY, INCLUDING FOOD, CLOTHING,
HOUSING, AND MEDICAL CARE AND NECESSARY
SOCIAL SERVICES.

— Article 25, Universal Declaration of Human Rights

"The border is in crisis. Texas state senators have declared it an emergency. One out of three persons live in poverty. Forty percent of schoolchildren live in poverty. The border has one of the nation's highest unemployment rates, at 11.4 percent."

GUILLERMO GLENN
Association of Border Workers

I am a member of the Border Workers Association in El Paso, Texas, which represents over 2,800 workers on the border in efforts to secure labor rights and help displaced workers fight for retraining and job replacement under the North American Free Trade Agreement (NAFTA).

In 1995, one year after NAFTA took effect, several electronic and health products manufacturing workers got together to figure out how we could save our jobs, as factories were closing down and moving at a rapid pace.

Communities across the country have been hit hard by loss of jobs due to free trade, but no other city has seen the effects as clearly as we have in El Paso. Since NAFTA, over 29,000 jobs have left El Paso, creating the largest number of NAFTA-displaced workers in the country. The city of El Paso estimates that each lost job costs $50,000/year in lost wages and sales revenue, totaling $1 billion lost by NAFTA-displaced workers alone.

And this trend continues. As of this March, 450 workers were laid off by Jones Apparel, 950 from Vanity Fair Jeans Corporation, 150 from International Garment Processor, and hundreds more from smaller factories. These were good-paying jobs that paid $12 or more per hour. It is no wonder that unemployment in El Paso is two to three times the state and national rates.

Before NAFTA was signed and implemented, a study was released by several research organizations that explained how the garment industry was going to leave El Paso due to NAFTA. The state, however, did nothing to prepare. They did not consider the workers and the diverse resources they would need to help displaced workers secure jobs. They should have implemented a bilingual job corps, eliminated discriminatory treatment toward Spanish speakers, and made resources available for economic development programs. But none of the above happened.

As part of NAFTA's Trade Adjustment Assistance Program, the Department of Labor gave a large grant to El Paso to provide job training to displaced workers. Eighty percent of the displaced workers in El Paso are Spanish speakers. However, no bilingual infrastructure was built to help displaced workers who were Spanish speaking. Without a GED and with limited English skills, the majority of these workers had very few options available to them. As a last resort, we filed a lawsuit in March 2002 against the Department of Labor and the Texas Workforce Development Board for denial of language and relevant job skills to workers in El Paso.

Those hardest hit by the restructuring are older Spanish-speaking factory workers—people defined by the marketplace as not worth training for new jobs, even if they are U.S. citizens. Spanish-speaking displaced workers have become the marginalized targets of harassment and discrimination in virtually all aspects of their lives.

Few programs exist to meet the needs of the thousands of workers who are being displaced. Yet existing workforce development funds do not provide resources to develop these programs. Instead, ineffective programs frequently continue to receive tuition and enrollees because of the pressure to enroll displaced workers in whatever program possible in order to maintain their eligibility for income support.

Since NAFTA, El Paso has experienced economic growth, but not everyone has shared the prosperity. Even the mayor of Juarez, just across the Mexican border from El Paso, recently remarked that NAFTA has been very beneficial for international corporations, but as the city "creates more and more wealth, [Juarez] becomes poorer and poorer."

The border is in crisis. Texas state senators have declared it an emergency. One out of three persons live in poverty. Forty percent of schoolchildren live in poverty. The border has one of the nation's highest unemployment rates, at 11.4 percent. We have seen record numbers of deaths caused by diabetes and hepatitis and other liver diseases.

With this kind of displacement and economic loss, neighborhoods and communities must be rebuilt. But how do we create jobs for American workers on the U.S. side of the border when corporations can now pay just one to two dollars an hour for labor right across the border?

It is imperative that displaced workers not be discarded as the inevitable losers in the destructive globalization process facilitated by so-called "free" trade agreements. Massive job loss is equivalent to a natural disaster; it has ramifications beyond the workers' lives, including damage to the community's social and economic fabric. Companies and corporations that displace workers should provide resources toward their reintegration into the workforce and the rebuilding of the community's economy and socioeconomic fabric. Trade adjustment resources are vital to ensuring that whole communities are not left behind in the new economy, but only if they are used in effective ways that genuinely help displaced workers and communities to rebuild their futures, rather than simply receiving a token handout.

THE FULL REALIZATION OF THIS RIGHT
[TO WORK] SHALL INCLUDE TECHNICAL AND
VOCATIONAL GUIDANCE AND TRAINING
PROGRAMS, POLICIES, AND TECHNIQUES TO
ACHIEVE STEADY ECONOMIC, SOCIAL,
AND CULTURAL DEVELOPMENT AND FULL AND
PRODUCTIVE EMPLOYMENT UNDER CONDITIONS
SAFEGUARDING FUNDAMENTAL POLITICAL
AND ECONOMIC FREEDOMS TO THE INDIVIDUAL.
— Article 6, International Covenant on Economic,
Social and Cultural Rights

# 3. Farm workers.

**"Farmworkers in the U.S. are displaced family farmers from Mexico, Guatemala, and Haiti, unable to compete with U.S. corporate agricultural giants. In this we share a great deal in common with U.S. family farmers."**

**LUCAS BENITEZ**
Coalition of Immokalee Workers

My name is Lucas Benitez. I left Mexico at seventeen, driven by the poverty that faces thousands of Mexicans. Although we work hard, work in our own fields no longer provides enough for food or clothing. My father is a peasant who always worked the land, growing corn (maize). But he had to stop because it is a crop that is no longer profitable and it was impossible to support a family on its harvest. My father had bigger dreams for his kids than for us to survive only on tortillas with salt and chile sauce to kill your hunger. So as soon as I could work on my own I left for the U.S. fields instead of joining my father in his fields as he did with his father. I came here with the idea of working hard to help my family. But the reality has been different.

I am a member of the Coalition of Immokalee Workers. We represent more than 2,500 low-wage workers based in the state of Florida who migrate along the entire East Coast of the U.S. The majority of us are immigrants from Mexico, Haiti, and Guatemala working in the agricultural industry. I myself am a farmworker in Immokalee, Florida, which is located in the heart of Florida's agricultural industry. In most ways, Immokalee is more of a labor reserve than a typical U.S. town—much like the communities of workers that developed around the South African diamond mines.

I say that for many reasons. We don't have just one boss or a sure job. Every day we wake up at 4:00 A.M. to go beg a day's work in the central parking lot in town. We may find work harvesting tomatoes today, picking oranges tomorrow, and doing maintenance at a golf course the next day. Or we might not have found any work at all. We earn subpoverty wages, receive absolutely no benefits, and are denied the right to overtime and to organize on the job. In fact, there have been five documented cases of modern-day slavery in Florida in the past five years alone. Yes, slavery.

Yet the Immokalee area is one of the most important agricultural areas of the United States, growing oranges, tomatoes, and other vegetables, a great many of which are used by fast food companies such as Taco Bell.

Thousands of us who find ourselves in Florida have been obligated to leave our countries because of the consequences of the free trade agreements that have flooded our countries' markets with cheap agricultural products from the United States and Canada, making it impossible for us to sell the crops that we have grown for generations.

That is why we as small peasant farmers in Latin America have seen ourselves displaced—no longer able to provide for our families by cultivating our own land. We who once grew our own food are now simply peons working for the huge multinational agribusinesses that are taking over and monopolizing the international agricultural market. In short, farmworkers in the U.S. are displaced family farmers from Mexico, Guatemala, and Haiti, unable to compete with U.S. corporate agricultural giants. In this we share a great deal in common with U.S. family farmers, who have themselves seen their livelihoods threatened by the overwhelming power of corporate agriculture.

And the conditions we find when we come to this country are worth repeating: subpoverty wages ($7,500 per year according to the U.S. Department of Labor), with no access to benefits like health insurance or overtime pay. In fact, over the past five years our organization, the Coalition of Immokalee Workers, has uncovered, investigated, and assisted the Department of Justice to prosecute five slavery rings that operated in Florida and up the East Coast. The last case concluded in November 2002, with three labor bosses who employed over 700 workers sentenced to twelve years each in federal prison for slavery, extortion, and firearms convictions.

Congressional support for expanding free trade means supporting unemployment and the exploitation of a workforce that benefits only a few multinational corporations. Though we don't have the money of the big corporations to contribute to your campaigns, we do have justice and human rights on our side, and we believe that justice should still count for something when important laws that will affect the lives of tens of millions of people are being signed. Human rights are universal. The right to an adequate standard of living is a right that should be guaranteed to family farmers and farmworkers around the world.

## NO ONE SHALL BE HELD IN SLAVERY OR SERVITUDE.

— Article 4, Universal Declaration of Human Rights

"We in this country, just like our counterparts in Mexico, are increasingly importing more and more of the food we consume. By doing so, we are ultimately placing the security of our food at risk and tearing apart the social fabric of our rural communities."

**DOLORES HUERTA**
United Farm Workers of America

The United Farm Workers of America, AFL-CIO, represents 43,000 farmworkers across the U.S. We have seen the devastating impact free trade has had on farmworkers, and we adamantly oppose any expansion of these agreements.

Free trade, as exemplified by NAFTA, has hurt hundreds of thousands of farmworkers here in the U.S. Since NAFTA, we have seen new waves of workers emigrating from the coffee growing regions of Veracruz, Mexico, where they were once small family coffee farmers. The free trade of coffee on the world market has destroyed the price coffee buyers once paid small family farmers. As a result, they are no longer able to support themselves and their families off the revenue generated from the coffee they grow, forcing them to leave their farms, risk their lives crossing the border to the U.S., and seek employment on farms in this country. Between 1995 and 2001, over 2,200 Mexicans died crossing the U.S. border. Those who survive find a situation not much different than what they left in Mexico.

This displacement is not only limited to coffee growers. It is estimated that 1.75 million Mexican nationals have been displaced due to free trade. Throughout Mexico, thousands of small family farmers grow corn for their own consumption and for sale within Mexico. These farmers, however, cannot compete with the corn from the U.S. In 2001, U.S. corn exporters dumped over five million tons of corn on the Mexican market at 25 percent below market cost. The Mexican government has reduced subsidies for corn production by 61 percent since NAFTA went into effect; meanwhile in the U.S., commodity payments continue to favor large multi-nationals that both grow and purchase corn and other grains from U.S. growers.

In the U.S., we have witnessed the dramatic decrease in the acreage of crops such as apples, asparagus, broccoli, cauliflower, mushrooms, grapes, and strawberries. In the last five years in the Willamette Valley of Oregon, three major food processors have closed their doors due to the availability of cheaper crops from other countries. In eastern Washington, the largest asparagus processor in the U.S. threatens to close, due in large part to the continued importation of tariff-free asparagus from Peru, which is far cheaper than asparagus grown locally.

The loss of acres of crops and the increasing number of food processors and packers who are closing up shop are wreaking havoc on rural communities throughout the U.S. Faced with the loss of buyers, growers are increasingly facing the real threat of bankruptcy and the loss of their family farms. Farmworkers, many of whom depended on jobs provided on the farms and in the processors and packing sheds, are now unemployed. In rural communities throughout the U.S., there is a scarcity of alternate jobs available to the increasing number of unemployed farmworkers and displaced U.S. farmers.

The net impact of these changes caused by free trade is that we in this country, just like our counterparts in Mexico, are importing more and more of the food we consume. We are ultimately placing the security of our food at risk and tearing apart the social fabric of our rural communities.

The continued expansion of unrestricted trade is not a given and inevitable. U.S. and Mexican agricultural policy can ensure the continued economic viability of family farmers by ensuring a fair playing field in the marketplace for all. But we must first work to remedy the damage that has been done by these free trade agreements and help family farmers from the U.S. and Mexico get back on their feet and earn a fair and just living from their dignified labor. The real human, social, and economic costs of free trade clearly indicate that U.S. trade negotiators should cease to sign any additional free trade agreements.

MIGRANT WORKERS AND MEMBERS OF THEIR FAMILIES SHALL HAVE THE RIGHT TO RECEIVE ANY MEDICAL CARE THAT IS URGENTLY REQUIRED FOR THE PRESERVATION OF THEIR LIFE OR THE AVOIDANCE OF IRREPARABLE HARM TO THEIR HEALTH ON THE BASIS OF EQUALITY OF TREATMENT WITH NATIONALS OF THE STATE CONCERNED. SUCH EMERGENCY MEDICAL CARE SHALL NOT BE REFUSED THEM BY REASON OF ANY IRREGULARITY WITH REGARD TO STAY OR EMPLOYMENT.

—Article 28, International Convention on the Protection of the Rights of All Migrant Workers and Members of Their Families

"Remembering that in many cases immigrant workers come to this country as a direct result of our own trade policies, we need to assess how America treats the strangers in our midst."

**BALDEMAR VELASQUEZ**

Farm Labor Organizing Committee

I was born in Pharr, Texas in 1947. My family was a typical migrant farmworker one, recruited to harvest tomatoes and sugar beets in Ohio and Michigan. All my life, my family and I endured low wages, bad working conditions, and housing that was more like barns and chicken coops than housing for people. After all these years of such severe conditions and labor abuses, we organized the Farm Labor Organizing Committee (FLOC) in 1967 to address the working and living conditions of farmworkers.

I am currently the president of FLOC, which represents approximately 7,000 migrant workers laboring in fifty-six separate family farms. Our membership consists of two different populations of workers who have similarly suffered a history of unjust economic policies that have created their conditions and predicament today.

One population is immigrant workers from Mexico whose livelihoods have been devastated by NAFTA. The small farmers and peasants of the Mexican countryside cannot compete with the relaxed import restrictions and subsidized American agriculture. The vast majority of these small farmers and their national organizations, like the Confederación Nacional Campesina (CNC), now oppose the current NAFTA terms and are calling for its renegotiations. Just to survive, many of these farmers have had to abandon their land and migrate to the United States to work for whatever dollars and in whatever conditions are offered to them.

Another population of FLOC's membership is Mexican-American citizens who have long been dispossessed of land. At the turn of the twentieth century, owners of the fertile land along the Rio Grande Valley had Latino surnames. In a short period of time, due to questionable practices of land development companies, ownership of those lands changed to people with Anglo surnames. The landless Mexican-American peoples, like our immigrant coworkers, had to migrate to find work. My own father and mother failed at sharecropping in South Texas before being recruited by a sugar beet growers association to come to Ohio to work in the sugar beet and tomato fields.

The conditions under which we work have worsened now under so-called "free" trade. It is imperative that our trade negotiators in the United States Trade Representative's Office stop ignoring minimum standards and rights to labor and the environment when they negotiate in the name of the American people. The current North American Free Trade Agreement has shown us that it has had a negative impact on the people we serve. It has weakened the rights of workers and worsened their working and living conditions, and it has devastated local economies.

Our immigration policies do no justice to the current trend of migration caused by free trade policies that force farmers in neighboring countries off their land. We need a modification of our immigration laws that would make it possible for our nation to do two things: one, to extend freedom of travel to those eight to nine million workers currently working in this country without documents, and let the labor market saturate itself; two, for security purposes, allow these eight to nine million workers to come out of hiding and document themselves so that our government can govern them.

More importantly, remembering that in many cases immigrant workers come to this country as a direct result of our own trade policies, we need to assess how America treats the strangers in our midst. Filling the void in the labor market in low-wage industries is one thing, but treating some to indentured servitude and, in some cases, slavery is immoral and unacceptable.

This is why we at FLOC have been proposing a just and fair immigration policy called the Freedom Act, which would legalize workers who are working and paying taxes and have not committed any crimes. This is why we boycott the Mt. Olive Pickle Company, because of their support of their suppliers' use of exploitable immigrant workers. Both of these efforts are important, because not only should our laws reflect justice for all, but our business practices should also not have to wait for laws to compel them to do what is right.

I would like to share a story about one of our farmworkers who recently died because he did not have rights as an immigrant worker. Thirty-two-year-old Urbano Ramirez was an undocumented worker harvesting cucumbers for one of the farms that supplied the Mt. Olive Pickle Company. One extremely hot, humid day, Urbano went to his supervisor and complained that he was not feeling well. He clearly exhibited symptoms of heatstroke. He had a bloody nose and nausea, and was fainting. He was denied medical help and was told to sit under a tree. At the end of the day, when the bus came to transport the workers back to the labor camp, Urbano was not under the tree, so the bus left without him. Two weeks later, his fellow workers, who had continued to look for him, discovered his body in a wooded area near the cucumber field, decomposed beyond recognition. He was identified by the IDs in his pocket, which also contained the chips representing the buckets of cucumbers he had picked that day. The punishment for the employer, which had failed to provide drinking water on that fateful day, was an $1,800 fine by the Department of Labor, for violation of the Federal Field Sanitation Standards.

As an American, I want to be able to tell the world that America indeed champions the human rights of all people abroad and at home. We must not allow injustices like Urbano's death and the oppression of millions of immigrant and migrant workers to persist because of the power of partisan money interests over the principles of freedom, liberty, and justice for all that made this country great.

[EVERYONE HAS THE RIGHT] TO
THE ENJOYMENT OF JUST AND FAVORABLE
CONDITIONS OF WORK WHICH ENSURE,
IN PARTICULAR...SAFE AND HEALTHY WORK
CONDITIONS.

— Article 7, International Covenant on Economic,
Social, and Cultural Rights

# 4. Ánalysts.

**" The definition of insanity is doing the same thing over and over and expecting a different result. Our current globalization policy is totally stark raving mad. "**

**LORI WALLACH**
Public Citizen's Global Trade Watch

Over the next year, Congress will be faced with decisions about new "trade" agreements with Chile, Singapore, and perhaps Central America. During this same period, U.S. trade negotiators will be trying to complete negotiations on the proposed thirty-one-nation NAFTA expansion known as the Free Trade Area of the Americas (FTAA) and on the Doha agenda of the World Trade Organization (WTO) expansion talks. If policymakers and the public are to have a reasonable basis for assessing the merits of future trade agreements, then it is essential that they have accurate data on the outcomes of past agreements and plausible estimates of the potential economic and other gains from liberalization, which can be balanced against the potential costs to the groups that are harmed.

The still-emerging system of corporate-led globalization is not a foregone conclusion. Despite the public relations efforts of those who benefit from this arrangement to convince us otherwise, the WTO and NAFTA agreements are merely one design; the model they put into practice is not inevitable. Nor is it representative of "free trade," a concept that people generally support. Rather, it is just one version of rules, which includes new kinds of protections. At stake with the blizzard of new proposed bilateral and regional free trade agreements, and with the WTO talks, is what model will be used.

I would emphasize that a focus on America's working poor is not a "protectionist" one. One can be pro-trade and internationalist and still demand transformative change to the current terms of globalization. Here in the U.S. and in other rich countries, we are late in coming to this critique relative to our counterparts in the global South, who have lived with the negative results of this model over the past thirty years under the policies of the International Monetary Fund (IMF) and World Bank. While the impact of this model on the livelihoods, food security, and environment of people in the global South far exceeds the impact on people living in the U.S., those who have been adversely impacted by this model have much in common, as evidenced by the international coalitions united in the pursuit of a more just and sustainable trade policy.

It's important to remember that these agreements are not just about trade. The WTO—and the sprawling rules that it enforces—actually covers a huge array of subjects not included in past agreements, including domestic food safety standards, environmental and product safety rules, service sector regulation, investment and development policy, intellectual property standards, government procurement rules, and more.

Almost ten years since NAFTA went into effect and almost nine years since the founding of the WTO, it is clear that the promised economic gains have not materialized, nor have environmental cleanups, lower food prices, or other benefits come to fruition. The main premise of this model is that liberalization will generate increased economic growth, therefore reducing poverty. A variety of studies and statistics are typically used to prove this has been the case. However, if one looks at the actual per capita income growth data from the World Bank—which uses per capita income growth to measure success—we can test this premise. Starting in the late 1970s, the World Bank imposed loan conditionalities, and the

IMF imposed "structural adjustment plans," which contained the same formula of policies and practices that the WTO, NAFTA, and proposed FTAA also forward. When we look at the data, what we see is that growth has slowed during the period when the current model was implemented. For instance, in Latin America, per capita income growth was 75 percent from 1960 to 1980, compared to an anemic 6 percent from 1980 to 1998. In sub-Saharan Africa, per capita income grew 36 percent in the first period, but in the latter period shrunk 15 percent.[2]

The decline in the quality of life for some of the most vulnerable populations worldwide does not translate into economic gains in the U.S. The working poor in the U.S. are losing, too:

- The 1999 UN Human Development Report found that in the wealthiest nations, job creation has lagged behind the growth in trade and investment volumes. In the U.S. from 1946 to 1973, there was an 80 percent gain in median wages. From 1972 to 2000, median wages were almost flat, even though international trade represented two times the share of U.S. economic activity that it did during the previous period.[3]

- During the round of trade negotiations that created the WTO, then-U.S. Treasury Secretary Lloyd

---

2 Mark Weisbrot, et al. Center for Economic Policy Research. *The Emperor Has No Growth: Declining Economic Growth Rates in the Era of Globalization*, 2001.
3 Mark Weisbrot. "Globalization for Dummies." *Harper's*, May 2000, 15.

Bentsen predicted that the passage of the round would result in an additional $1,700 in annual income per U.S. family. But the median family income has not risen by $1,700 per year during any of the past eight years, despite the fact that the U.S. had a period of unprecedented economic growth.[4]

- The service sector and high-tech jobs that we were told would be our employment future are beginning to follow the manufacturing jobs to low-wage countries, with more than 3 million U.S. jobs expected to be shifted to China and other nations by 2015.[5] Meanwhile, the Department of Labor says that the employment categories that will have the most future growth (besides a few categories of computer specialists and engineers) are home health aids, personal care aids, and security guards[6]—meaning even greater threats for the 74 percent of the American workforce without a college degree.[7]

- The U.S. also lost 38,310 small farms between 1995 and 2002.[8] NAFTA and the WTO required coun-

---

4 Lloyd Bentsen. "The Uruguay Round—Now." Washington Post, September 13, 1994, A21.
5 Peter S. Goodman. "White-Collar Work: A Booming U.S. Export."
Washington Post, April 2, 2003.
6 U.S. Department of Labor, Bureau of Labor Statistics. 2000–2010 Employment Projections.
7 U.S. Department of Commerce, Census Bureau. "The Big Payoff: Educational Attainment and Synthetic Estimates of Work-Life Earnings," July 2002, 2.
8 USDA, National Agricultural Statistics Service. "Farms and Farm Land in Farms 2002," February 2003, 1.

tries to eliminate the programs that safeguard small farmers against predatory commodity traders and fluky weather. As a result, the six grain trading giants who now control three-quarters of all world grain trade[9] have been able to manipulate supply and prices, meaning that the prices paid to farmers for their commodities are at an all-time low—and below the cost of production. At the same time, the consumer price index for food in the U.S. rose by 19.8 percent between 1993 and 2000.[10]

This snapshot of some of the economic outcomes skims over the many other problems these pacts have caused America's working poor. Health and environmental problems related to service sector liberalization and environmental and health deregulation have hit America's poor the hardest. When the WTO ruled against the U.S. Clean Air Act regulations in 1997, the weakening of that standard meant that in America's most polluted cities, gasoline cleanliness standards were dropped, threatening more illness—especially asthma—for America's inner-city kids. And I could go on and on....

The bottom line: the definition of insanity is doing the same thing over and over and expecting a different result. Our current globalization policy is totally stark raving mad. We

---

9 Mary Hendrickson and William Heffernan. "Concentration of Agriculture Markets." Department of Rural Sociology, University of Missouri, February 2002.
10 Bureau of Labor Statistics. "Consumer Price Index for All Food at Home, U.S. City Average," series ID CUSR0000SAFF11, extracted June 7, 2001.

need to transform this lose-lose model into a set of global rules that will regulate multinational corporations and the excesses of the market to ensure a more just, sustainable, and democratically accountable system that meets human needs in the rich and poor countries alike.

**Employers have been using the threat of capital mobility with increasing frequency to effectively hold down wages and restrain workers from organizing.**

**KATE BRONFENBRENNER**
School of Industrial and Labor Relations,
Cornell University

tarting in 1988 and continuing to the present, I have conducted a series of studies specifically designed to gain greater insight into factors contributing to the impact of capital mobility and threats of capital mobility on workers, wages, and unions.[11]

For more than a decade, there has been a great deal of discussion regarding the possible implications that U.S. trade agreements such as NAFTA, Permanent Normal Trade Relations with China (PNTR), and FTAA might have for the U.S. economy, particularly wages and employment for U.S. workers. Today these questions become even more critical as trade deficit figures approach record highs, and hundreds of thousands of well-paying jobs in some of the nation's largest and most profitable companies leave the U.S. for Mexico, China, and other countries.

What our last fifteen years of research has shown is that there is a clear pattern in operation; namely that production shifts and threats of production shifts out of the country esca-

---

11 Kate Bronfenbrenner, et al. "The Impact of US-China Trade Relations on Workers, Wages, and Employment: Pilot Study Report." Commissioned research paper and supplement to *Report to Congress of the US-China Security Review Commission: The National Security Implications of the Economic Relationship Between the United States and China.* Washington, D.C.: US-China Security Review Commission, 2002. Kate Bronfenbrenner. "Uneasy Terrain. The Impact of Capital Mobility on Workers, Wages, and Union Organizing." Commissioned research paper and supplement to *The U.S. Trade Deficit: Causes, Consequences and Recommendations for Action,* Washington, D.C.: U.S. Trade Deficit Review Commission, November, 2000. Kate Bronfenbrenner. "The Effect of Plant Closings and the Threat of Plant Closings on Worker Rights to Organize." Supplement to *Plant Closings and Workers Rights: A Report to the Council of Ministers by the Secretariat of the Commission for Labor Cooperation,* Dallas, Tex.: Bernan Press, June, 1997. Kate Bronfenbrenner, Sheldon Friedman, Richard Hurd, Rudy Oswald, and Ron Seeber, eds. *Organizing to Win: New Research on Union Strategies.* Ithaca, N.Y.: ILR Press, January 1998. Kate Bronfenbrenner. "Employer Behavior in Certification Elections and First Contracts: Implications for Labor Law Reform." In Sheldon Friedman, Richard Hurd, Rudy Oswald, and Ronald Seeber, eds. *Restoring the Promise of American Labor Law.* Ithaca NY: ILR Press, 1994. Kate Bronfenbrenner and Tom Juravich. "The Impact of Employer Opposition on Union Certification Win Rates: A Private/Public Comparison." Economic Policy Institute Working Paper No. 113, 1995.

late in the aftermath of each new trade and investment agreement. Equally important, we have found that employers have been using the threat of capital mobility with increasing frequency to effectively hold down wages and restrain workers from organizing.

We have also found that the recent acceleration in capital mobility has had a devastating impact on the extent and nature of union organizing campaigns. Where employers can credibly threaten to shut down and/or move their operations in response to union activity, they do so in large numbers. Overall, more than half of all employers made threats to close all or part of their operations during an organizing drive. The threat rate is significantly higher, 71 percent, in the manufacturing sector, compared to a 36 percent threat rate in relatively immobile industries such as construction, health care, education, retail, and other services. This contrasts sharply with the late 1980s, before NAFTA, when only 29 percent of all employers made plant-closing threats during organizing campaigns.

Our research has found that not only are threats of plant closing an extremely pervasive part of employer campaigns, they are also very effective. The National Labor Relations Board certification election win rate associated with campaigns where the employer made plant closing threats is, at 38 percent, significantly lower than the 51 percent win rate found in units where no threats occurred. Win rates were lowest, averaging only 32 percent, in campaigns with threats in mobile industries such as manufacturing, communications, and wholesale distribution, where the threats are more credible.

We also found threats of plant closing to be unrelated to the financial condition of the company, with threats no less likely to occur in companies in a stable financial condition than in those on the edge of bankruptcy. Instead, threats seemed to be primarily motivated by employer antiunion animus—just another tactic in their antiunion campaigns, one that very effectively plays on the real fears of workers living and working in an increasingly mobile economy.

But the impact of trade and investment policy and capital mobility on workers and wages goes well beyond the union organizing process. Each day U.S. workers need only pick up the newspaper or turn on the news to hear yet another story of a major company shifting operations or threatening to shift operations to Mexico, China, or other countries. In fact, in just the first seven months after PNTR was passed by Congress in October of 2000, our research found that more than eighty corporations announced their intentions to shift production to China, with the number of announced production shifts increasing each month, from two per month in October to nineteen per month by April. The number of jobs that the major media estimated were lost through these production shifts was as high as 34,900, fourteen percent of which were in unionized facilities. During this same period, another 148 corporations announced plans to shift production to Mexico, covering another 29,000 jobs, 48 percent of which were union. However, these were just production shifts and job losses announced in the major media. According to our estimates, the actual number of jobs lost through production shifts to China and Mexico averages between 70,000 and 100,000 jobs each year.

The U.S. companies that are shutting down and moving out of the country tend to be large, profitable, well-established companies. They are primarily subsidiaries of publicly held, U.S.-based multinationals, including such familiar names as Mattel, International Paper, General Electric, Motorola, and Rubbermaid. Most have been in operation for nearly half a century, and many are unionized. Many of those who lose their jobs are high-seniority, top-of-the-pay-scale employees who have a great deal invested in their jobs and in their communities.

The employment effects of these production shifts go well beyond the individual workers whose jobs are lost. Each time another company shuts downs operations and moves work to China, Mexico, or any other country, it has a ripple effect on the wages of every other worker in that industry and that community, through lowering wage demands, restraining union organizing and bargaining power, reducing the tax base, and reducing or eliminating hundreds of jobs in the related contracting, transportation, wholesale trade, professional, and service-sector employment in companies and businesses.

What these data show is that the U.S. and other countries have moved ahead with trade policies and global economic integration based on false assumptions about the impact those policies would have on employment and wages in the U.S. Rather than strengthening our economy, these policies are pushing wages down for all workers, and pushing more and more families and communities into poverty.

In conclusion, our research suggests three paths to break

the hold that capital mobility has on the economic confidence and security of America's workers. The first is the establishment of trade and tax policies that incorporate strong and enforceable labor standards in trade agreements and provide disincentives to companies that seek to move employment out of the country, in particular in response to union campaigns. The second requires changes in U.S. laws to require employer neutrality in the organizing process and provide for substantial financial penalties and injunctive relief for the most egregious employer interference with workers exercising their right to organize. The third points to the critical need for government-mandated corporate reporting on production, trade, and investment flows in and out of the U.S., and for holding off on further trade agreements until we have accurate and complete data on the impact of trade policies on workers, unions, families, and communities in the U.S. and around the globe.

" In Mexico real wages are actually lower than before NAFTA was put in place, and the number of people in poverty has grown. "

**THEA LEE**

American Federation of Labor and Congress of Industrial Organizations (AFL-CIO)

"Free trade" has been sold to the American public and American workers as a cure for all that ails us. Proponents of so-called free trade—regional agreements like the North American Free Trade Agreement (NAFTA), World Trade Organization (WTO) negotiations, and the granting of permanent normal trade relations to China (PNTR)—have claimed that these agreements would create high-paying export-related jobs here in the United States, bring prosperity to developing countries, and spur economic growth and political stability worldwide. The outcome has been quite different.

Since NAFTA and the WTO were put in place (1994 and 1995, respectively), the United States has lost over 3 million jobs, according to estimates by the Economic Policy Institute,[12] which calculates the employment impact of changes in the U.S. trade balance. Meanwhile, "free trade" has brought mixed results to many developing countries— often spurring growth in investment and trade flows, but not always improving wages and working conditions for the typical worker or small farmer. And global economic growth has slowed, not accelerated, in the last two decades of increased trade and capital liberalization (compared to the previous two decades, 1960 to 1980).[13]

The U.S. trade deficit in goods hit an all-time record of $484 billion in 2002, meaning that we imported almost half a

---

12 Robert E. Scott. "Phony Accounting and U.S. Trade Policy." *Economic Policy Institute Issue Brief* No. 184, October 23, 2002.
13 Mark Weisbrot, Dean Baker, Egor Kraev, and Judy Chen. "The Scorecard on Globalization 1980-2000: Twenty Years of Diminished Progress." Center for Economic and Policy Research, July 11, 2001.

trillion dollars-worth more goods than we exported. A trade deficit of this magnitude stems from national economic policies that have utterly failed in almost every dimension: U.S. trade and tax policies encourage and reward companies that move jobs overseas to take advantage of workers who are denied their basic human rights; the overvalued dollar puts domestic producers at an impossible disadvantage; and unfair trade practices by other countries keep our goods out of overseas markets.

The overall trade deficit (in both goods and services) represents a drag of 4.2 percent on U.S. economic growth, slowing any possibility of strong economic recovery and undermining future job growth. The high import propensity of the U.S. economy means that even as economic recovery gets under way, a large proportion of every dollar spent by consumers goes to purchase imports, undermining the economy's ability to generate good jobs at home.

These figures are very real to working Americans, who are losing family-supporting jobs and benefits as manufacturing and even service jobs are lost overseas.

U.S. goods exports actually fell in 2001 and in 2002, exposing the falsehood in the administration's cheerleading that current U.S. trade policies are enhancing our competitiveness in overseas markets. In 2002, total U.S. goods exports were only $694 billion, down almost $90 billion from the 2000 level.

This year's trade figures also reveal other startling weaknesses in the U.S. economy, even in those areas that have traditionally been considered U.S. strongholds, like services and advanced technology products. The trade surplus in services plunged by almost $20 billion in 2002, from $68 billion to $49 billion. In advanced technology products, similarly, the U.S. surplus of $4.5 billion in 2001 turned into a whopping deficit of $17.5 billion last year. These trends call into question the conventional wisdom that the United States enjoys a permanent and growing comparative advantage in the export of services and high technology goods.

In general, the experience of our unions and our members with past trade agreements has led us to question critically the extravagant claims often made on their behalf. While these agreements are inevitably touted as market-opening agreements that will significantly expand U.S. export opportunities (and therefore create export-related U.S. jobs), the impact has more often been to facilitate the shift of U.S. investment offshore. (As these agreements contain far-reaching protections for foreign investors, it is clear that facilitating the shift of investment is an integral goal of these "trade" agreements.) Much, although not all, of this investment has gone into production for export back to the United States, boosting U.S. imports and displacing rather than creating U.S. jobs.

The net impact has been a negative swing in our trade balance with every single country with which we have negotiated a free trade agreement (FTA) to date. While we understand that many other factors influence bilateral trade balances (including most notably growth trends and exchange rate movements), it is nonetheless striking that none of the FTAs we have signed to date has yielded an improved bilateral trade balance (including agreements with Israel, Canada, Mexico, and Jordan).

The case of the North American Free Trade Agreement (NAFTA) is both the most prominent and the most striking. Advocates of NAFTA promised better access to 90 million consumers on our southern border and prosperity for Mexico, yielding a "win-win" outcome. Yet in nine years of NAFTA, our combined trade deficit with Mexico and Canada has ballooned from $9 billion to $87 billion. The Labor Department has certified that more than half a million U.S. workers have lost their jobs due to NAFTA, while the Economic Policy Institute puts the trade-related job losses at over 700,000. Meanwhile, in Mexico real wages are actually lower than before NAFTA was put in place, and the number of people in poverty has grown.

Since Congress granted China permanent normal trade relations in 2000 (and China acceded to the rules of the WTO), the U.S. trade deficit with China has grown by almost 25 percent, hitting a staggering $103 billion last year—our single largest bilateral deficit. Meanwhile, the Chinese government continues to arrest and brutally repress workers who advocate for independent unions or better working conditions.[14]

If the goal of these so-called "free trade" agreements is truly to open foreign markets to American exports (and not to reward and encourage companies that shift more jobs overseas), it is pretty clear the strategy is not working. Before

---

[14] See Human Rights Watch's press release and indictment at www.hrw.org/press/2003/02/china021403.htm.

Congress approves new bilateral free trade agreements based on an outdated model, it is imperative that we take some time to figure out how and why the current policy has failed.

The AFL-CIO believes that increased international trade and investment, if done right, can yield broad and substantial benefits, both to American working families and to our brothers and sisters around the world. Trade agreements must include enforceable protections for core workers' rights and must preserve our ability to use our domestic trade laws effectively. They must protect our government's ability to regulate in the public interest, to use procurement dollars to promote economic development and other legitimate social goals, and to provide high-quality public services. Finally, it is essential that workers, their unions, and other civil society organizations be able to participate meaningfully in our government's trade policy process, on an equal footing with corporate interests.

Unfortunately, we see little evidence that this administration has learned from the mistakes of past, failed trade policies. It is determined to replicate these mistakes in the Free Trade Area of the Americas and the bilateral and regional agreements presently being negotiated. If we do not dramatically reform these failed trade policies, soon many more Americans will be among the "working poor."

"Trade policy is less accessible and accountable to the people of each nation and more accessible and responsive to multinational corporations that do not see themselves as citizens of any particular country."

ANNA BLACKSHAW

California Senate Select Committee on
International Trade Policy and State Legislation

The Select Committee on International Trade Policy and State Legislation was created three years ago by the California Senate as a result of concerns that international trade rules could seriously impair the ability of state and local lawmakers to address matters of public interest to their citizens.

As the fifth-largest economy in the world, and as a national and global leader on issues of economic development, labor and human rights standards, consumer protections, and environmental sustainability, we are deeply concerned that as the reach of international trade rules and sanctions expands, the traditional plenary power of the states in our federal system as the principal guardians of the health, safety, and welfare of their citizens could contract, undermining more than two centuries of American constitutional values.

While we believe that increased international trade and investment is of critical importance to California, and can yield substantial benefits, we feel it imperative that trade agreements must not only preserve the efficacy of our long-standing republican and democratic institutions, and hence our ability to debate, craft, and pass legislation in the public interest, but must also include enforceable protections for workers' rights and environmental sustainability. It is also essential that state and local legislators, unions, NGOs, and civil society have an opportunity to engage in a meaningful and significant manner in the making of international trade policies.

Unfortunately, the Chile and Singapore Free Trade Agreements, which will soon come before Congress, fall short of these benchmarks, as do current negotiations of the General Agreement on Trade in Services (GATS), the Free Trade Area of the Americas (FTAA), and the Central American Free Trade Agreement (CAFTA).

These agreements contain the troubling NAFTA investor-to-state provisions which grant private foreign investors extraordinary powers to challenge legitimate government actions when the profits of such investors are diminished by state or local environmental laws, consumer protection statutes, or judicial decrees. California witnessed this first-hand when the Canadian corporation Methanex challenged our phaseout of the gasoline additive MTBE, a possible car-cinogen. Using these investor-to-state rules, Methanex, the makers of one component of MTBE, was able to claim that the California action was a confiscation of its property—its expected profit—and sued for $1 billion. In spite of the trade act of 2002, which directed trade negotiators to ensure that foreign investors were given no greater rights than U.S. investors, current investment language contains large loop-holes that allow these protections to still stand. This, despite the fact that a broad coalition of state legislators, state chief justices, city officials, mayors, and attorneys general asked Congress to provide safeguards to prevent this abuse.

We are also very concerned about negotiations to open up U.S. private and public service sectors to competition by for-eign companies. The services agenda includes a broad scope of areas, such as the privatization and deregulation of public water and energy utilities, health care, and postal services, and the deregulation of private sector service industries such as banking, mutual funds, and insurance. For example, the proposed rules on "domestic regulation" could allow foreign corporations or governments to challenge a wide array of California health care regulations as "more burdensome than necessary." This could include nurse-to-patient staffing ratios and professional licensing standards. Living wage laws and project labor agreements—labor laws intended to ensure rights for workers—could be subject to challenge under these provisions.

Having so recently experienced vast problems with electricity deregulation and the deregulation of worker's compensation rates—both of which have led to full blown crises in California—Californians have reason to be particularly wary of such an agenda.

The very architecture of these agreements seems designed to limit the constitutionally grounded authority and traditional role and processes of state-based governance, turning on its head the deeply embedded notion that under our federalist system, states are the primary protectors of the health, safety, and welfare of their citizens, and are thus invested with plenary powers to address these fundamental concerns. Under these new models of international trade, local government accountability and public protection take a backseat to the ideologically driven agendas of deregulation and privatization, which would sweepingly decree any legislation that might be viewed as hostile to these policy preferences as an unfair barrier to the natural laws of the free market. The resulting trade policy is less accessible and accountable to the people of each nation and more accessible and responsive to multinational corporations that do not see themselves as citizens of any particular country.

Our hard-fought-for laws and standards in California reflect our values about the kind of state we want to live in. They exist because legislators and citizens together identified meaningful ways to improve the conditions in which we live. We believe deeply in them, and in our right to enact them. Trade agreements that undermine this process jeopardize the public welfare and pose grave consequences for democracy here and throughout the world. Trade agreements should harmonize our standards upward, not downward, and they must respect democracy and citizen participation at every step. Trade, as important and as valuable as it is, should not be valued above our hard-won, long-cherished, self-governing freedoms.

# RESOURCES

The following individuals and organizations contributed essays to this book.

**American Corn Growers Association**
53495 840 Rd
Tilden, NE 68781
Phone: 402-368-7786
Fax: 402-368-2114
www.acga.org

The American Corn Growers Association is America's leading progressive commodity association, representing 14,000 corn producers in 28 states. Founded in 1987, the ACGA has worked for national farm legislation that provides a fair price from the marketplace to corn producers.

**American Federation of Labor-Congress of Industrial Organizations (AFL-CIO)**
815 16th Street, N.W.
Washington, DC 20006
Phone: 202-637-5000
Fax: 202-637-5058
www.aflcio.org

The AFL-CIO is an alliance of America's unions, which includes 65 member unions and 13 million workers. Its mission is to bring social and economic justice to the United States by enabling working people to have a voice on the job, in government, in a changing global economy and in their communities.

### Asociación de Trabajadores Fronterizos (Association of Border Workers)

P.O. Box 10454
El Paso, TX 79995
Phone: 915-533-6929
www.atfelpaso.org

The Association of Border Workers is a community-based organization that helps to empower Spanish-speaking workers who have been laid off in El Paso because of NAFTA and other free trade agreements.

### Black Farmers and Agriculturalists Association

P.O. Box 61
Tillery, NC 27887
Phone: 252-826-2800
Fax: 252-826-3244
http://www.coax.net/people/lwf/bfaa.htm

The BFAA is a grassroots, volunteer organization with chapters in 21 states. It was founded in 1997 to stop the extinction of African-American farmers and landowners.

### Dr. Kate Bronfenbrenner

New York State School of Industrial and Labor Relations
Cornell University
119 Ives Hall
Ithaca, NY 14853

Phone: 607-255-7581
Fax: 607-255-0245

## John Bunting
Dairy farmer and member of the NFFC
2362 Peakes Brook Road
Delhi, NY 13753
Phone: 607-746-3892
bunting@delhi.net

## Chinese Progressive Association (CPA)
1042 Grant Avenue, 5th Floor
San Francisco, CA 94133
Phone: 415-391-6986
Visit their sister website at: www.cpaboston.org

The Chinese Progressive Association is a grassroots membership organization in the San Francisco Bay Area that works to improve the living and working conditions of Chinese-Americans and empower community members to make decisions that affect their lives.

## Coalition of Immokalee Workers (CIW)
P.O. Box 603
Immokalee, Fl 34143
Phone: 239-657-8311
Fax: 239-657-8311
www.ciw-online.org

The CIW is a community-based worker organization largely composed of Latino, Haitian, and Mayan Indian immigrants. They have been fighting to end indentured servitude in the fields and for improved wages, better working conditions, decent and affordable housing, and the enforcement of labor laws, such as the right to organize.

### Farm Labor Organizing Committee (FLOC)
1221 Broadway
Toledo, OH 43609
Phone: 419-243-3456
Fax: 419-243-5655
www.floc.com

The Farm Labor Organizing Committee (FLOC) of AFL-CIO is a union representing people who do some of the most important work in America—migrant farmworkers who pick the food we eat. Since its formation in 1968, FLOC has organized farmworkers for better wages, living conditions, and workers' and immigrants' rights.

### Fuerza Unida
710 Nuevo Laredo Highway
San Antonio, TX 78211
Phone: 210-927-2294
Fax: 210-927-2295
http://fuerzaunida.freeservers.com/

Fuerza Unida was formed when thousands of workers were laid off from Levi Strauss & Company. They organized a successful national boycott of the popular jeans company and a visible 21-day hunger strike at the Levi's headquarters in San Francisco.

## International Longshoremen's Association

ILA Local 1422

910 Morrison Drive

Charleston, SC 29403

http://ilaunion.org/

The International Longshoremen's Association, AFL-CIO, is the largest union of maritime workers in North America, representing upwards of 65,000 longshoremen on the Atlantic and Gulf Coasts, Great Lakes, major U.S. rivers, Puerto Rico, and Eastern Canada.

## National Family Farm Coalition (NFFC)

110 Maryland Avenue, N.E., Suite 307

Washington, DC 20002

Phone: 202-543-5675

Fax: 202-543-0978

www.nffc.net

The NFFC was founded in 1986 to bring together farmers and others to strengthen family farms and rural communities. NFFC organizes national projects focused on preserving and strengthening family farms and serves as a network for groups opposing corporate agriculture. Membership currently consists of 33 grassroots farm, resource conservation, and rural advocacy groups from 33 states.

## Pacific Coast Federation of Fishermen's Associations (PCFFA)

P.O. Box 29370

San Francisco, CA 94129

Phone: 415-561-5080
Fax: 415-561-5464
www.pcffa.org/

The PCFFA is the largest and most politically active trade association of commercial fishermen in the U.S. For the last 20 years, they have been leading the industry in assuring the rights of individual fishermen and fighting for the long-term survival of commercial fishing as a productive livelihood. PCFFA is a federation of 25 port and fishermen's associations that spans the West Coast from San Diego to Alaska.

**Public Citizen**
**Global Trade Watch**
1600 20th Street, NW
Washington, DC 20009
Phone: 202-588-1000
www.citizen.org/trade

Global Trade Watch (GTW) is a division of Public Citizen, a national consumer and environmental group founded in 1972 by Ralph Nader with about 250,000 dues-paying members mainly in the U.S. GTW was created in 1995 to promote government and corporate accountability in the globalization and trade arena.

**United Farm Workers of America (UFW)**
P.O. Box 62
Keene, CA 93531
www.ufw.org

Founded in 1962 by Cesar Chavez and Dolores Huerta, the

UFW was the first farm-labor union in the United States. For 40 years, the UFW has fought to organize farmworkers, raise wages, improve working conditions, and win collective bargaining, legal, and legislative protections for farmworkers, the poorest and most abused workers in the United States.

**California Senate Select Committee on International Trade Policy and State Legislation**

1020 N Street #551

Sacramento, CA 95814

Phone: 916-322-8616

Fax: 916-324-3036

http://www.senate.ca.gov/ftp/sen/committee/select/INTER_TRADE/_home/

This committee weighs the impacts of international trade agreements on California laws and explores the appropriate relationships between states and the federal government when international trade policy intersects with traditional state roles in environmental protection, natural resource management, human rights protections, and public safety.

# ABOUT FOOD FIRST

F ood First, also known as the Institute for Food and Development Policy, is a nonprofit research and education-for-action center dedicated to investigating and exposing the root causes of hunger in a world of plenty. It was founded in 1975 by Frances Moore Lappé, author of the bestseller Diet for a Small Planet, and food policy analyst Dr. Joseph Collins. Food First research has revealed that hunger is created by concentrated economic and political power, not by scarcity. Resources and decision-making are in the hands of a wealthy few, depriving the majority of land, jobs, and therefore food.

Hailed by the New York Times as "one of the most established food think tanks in the country," Food First has grown to profoundly shape the debate about hunger and development.

But Food First is more than a think tank. Through books, reports, videos, media appearances, and speaking engagements, Food First experts not only reveal the often hidden roots of hunger, they show how individuals can get involved in bringing an end to the problem. Food First inspires action by bringing to light the courageous efforts of people around the world who are creating farming and food systems that truly meet people's needs.

## BECOME A MEMBER OF FOOD FIRST

Private contributions and membership gifts form the financial base of Food First. The success of the Institute's programs depends not only on its dedicated volunteers and staff, but on financial activists as well. Each member strengthens Food First's efforts to change a hungry world. We invite you to join Food First. As a member you will receive a 20 percent discount on all Food First books. You will also receive our quarterly publication, *Food First News and Views*, and timely *Backgrounders* that provide information and suggestions for action on current food and hunger crises in the United States and around the world. If you want to subscribe to our Internet newsletters, *Food Rights Watch* and *We Are Fighting Back*, send us an email at foodfirst@foodfirst.org. All contributions are tax-deductible.

## BECOME AN INTERN FOR FOOD FIRST

There are opportunities for interns in research, advocacy, campaigning, publishing, computers, media, and publicity at Food First. Our interns come from around the world. They are a vital part of our organization and make our work possible.

To become a member or apply to become an intern, just call, visit our web site, or clip and return the attached coupon to

Food First/Institute for Food and Development Policy
398 60th Street, Oakland, CA 94618, USA
PHONE 510.654.4400 / FAX 510.654.4551
EMAIL foodfirst@foodfirst.org
WEB www.foodfirst.org

# JOINING FOOD FIRST

---

☐ I want to join Food First. Enclosed is my tax-deductible contribution of:

☐ $35  ☐ $50  ☐ $100  ☐ $1,000  ☐ Other

Name _____

Address _____

City/State/Zip _____

Daytime phone _____

Email _____

You are also invited to give a gift membership to others interested in the fight to end hunger.

## GIFT MEMBERSHIPS

---

☐ Enclosed is my tax-deductible contribution of:

☐ $35  ☐ $50  ☐ $100  ☐ $1,000  ☐ Other

Please send a Food First membership to:

Name _____

Address _____

City/State/Zip _____

From _____

# ABOUT FOOD FIRST BOOKS

Food First books are credible, cogent, progressive books on timely topics. Food First Books is the publishing arm of the Institute for Food and Development Policy/Food First, a member-supported think tank on food and social justice issues. Food First was established in 1975 by Frances Moore Lappé, author of the revolutionary bestseller *Diet for a Small Planet*, and Joseph Collins, and has been called "one of the most established food think tanks in the country" by the *New York Times*. We are in the forefront of progressive research and action in the areas of free trade, biotechnology, the global food system, and economic human rights.

For a catalog, or to order a book, check out our website, www.foodfirst.org, or drop us a line at

Food First Books
Catalog Request
398 60th Street
Oakland, CA 94618, USA
FAX: 510-654-4551
EMAIL: foodfirst@foodfirst.org

If you are a bookseller or other reseller, contact our distributor, CDS, at 800-343-4499, to order.